SOCCER WORLD
SPAIN

Explore the World Through Soccer

Ethan Zohn & David Rosenberg

Illustrated by Chad Thompson

ACKNOWLEDGMENTS

Ethan would like to dedicate this book to the future soccer stars of the Zohn family: Ava, Adin, Oliver, Isaiah, and Zoe; Jenna Morasca for all her love and loyalty; my awesome mom, Rochelle, for her encouragement and teaching me how to be a creative writer; Lenard and Lee Zohn for being the best brothers ever; and David Rosenberg for his expertise, guidance, and making this book happen. To Nomad Press for all their support; all the staff, volunteers, interns, and students of Grassroot Soccer; and to all the selfless warriors out there fighting to put an end to cancer.

David thanks Gael Richard Sydness for sharing his adopted country; Ellen Harrigan, Karen Marrs, Joseph Serino, Jason Crockett, Dan Puglisi, Michael Reza, Marius Bratoiu, and Rebecca Sinclair; Robert and Cooper Ulrich, Lane Carlson, and Jon and Lisa Seda for their open hearts; and Scott Elrod and Mats Christeen for small acts of remarkable kindness. There would be no book without Ethan's amazing spirit, and the love of my wife Suzanne Kent. This book is dedicated to Andrew, Mark, and Deb Greenberg and to the memory of Harrison James Greenberg, who lived his 20 years with great grace.

This book was manufactured by Transcontinental Interglobe,
Beauceville Quebec, Canada
April 2011, Job# 53023
ISBN: 978-1-9363133-6-5

Illustrations by Chad Thompson

Questions regarding the ordering of this book should be addressed to
Independent Publishers Group
814 N. Franklin St.
Chicago, IL 60610
www.ipgbook.com

Nomad Press
2456 Christian St.
White River Junction, VT 05001
www.nomadpress.net

INTRODUCTION
Meet Ethan
1

Glossary Index

MEET ETHAN

WHO'S READY FOR AN EXCITING ADVENTURE?

My name is Ethan Zohn and I have loved soccer since I was six years old. As a professional player I have played all over the world. My favorite matches were in South Africa, Argentina, Canada, and Australia, just to name a few.

Soccer is played in almost every nation. This game is like a common language that brings people together. I can just show up at a field with a ball and make 20 cool new friends.

"Soccer is called football in other countries"

How would you like to join me on my *Soccer World* adventures? We will meet kids just like you. They will share their culture with us, from favorite foods to cool places to visit. They will even teach us a word or two in their language.

We'll go to some amazing places and even meet some native animals. Along the way, we'll discover some fun activities that you can do in your classroom or at home.

What are you waiting for? Grab your soccer ball. Let's begin our journey through Spain!

VISIT ME!

Because you are my travel buddy, you can go to my website. See photos of the places we visit and find more activities and projects at www.soccerworldadventure.com.

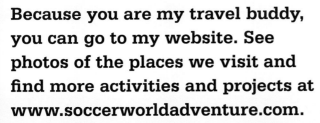

2

THE SPIRIT OF SPAIN

We are riding on a ship towards Barcelona. This is one of the main cities of Spain. I am very excited to share this adventure with you. We are heading to a unique country—a country that proudly won the 2010 FIFA World Cup, which was played in the nation of South Africa.

Europe

France

Portugal

Spain

Mediterranean Sea

Africa

Spain sits on the Iberian **peninsula** in southwestern Europe. It is bigger in land size than California. Spain is bordered on the north by France and Andorra, and on the west by Portugal. There are 50 Spanish **provinces**, the same number of states that we have in America.

WORDS 2 KNOW

peninsula: a piece of land that juts out into water.

province: part of a country.

Phoenicians: people who explored the Mediterranean Sea 3,000 years ago.

port: a harbor where ships can load and unload.

Since Spain is surrounded by water, it made the country an important stop when ships explored the world. The ancient **Phoenicians** and Greeks had **ports** in Spain.

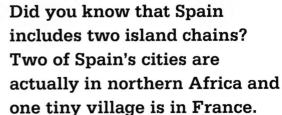

Did you know that Spain includes two island chains? Two of Spain's cities are actually in northern Africa and one tiny village is in France.

Both the ancient Romans and North Africans ruled Spain at different times. Because of this, many different countries have influenced its **customs** and **culture**.

"**Spain's experiences with outside cultures have made it a land of many traditions.**"

customs: ways of doing things.

culture: the beliefs and customs of a group of people.

traditions: customs handed down over time.

democracy: government elected freely by the people.

autonomous: independent.

Today Spain is a **democracy**. It has 17 regions, called **autonomous** communities, that have their own languages and celebrations.

Spanish is the official language. There are four official co-languages. Several others are also recognized by the government. We will experience this as we travel around the country.

THE NAME IN SPAIN

Learn to say "My name is" in some of the different languages of Spain.

SPANISH
Mi nombre es [your name]
(mee NOM-bray es)

ARAGONESE
Mi clamo [your name]
(mee CLAM-o)

ASTURIAN
El mio nome ye or
Llámome [your name]
(el MEE-o NO-may e)
(YAHM-mo-may)

BASQUE *
Nire izena [your name] da
(NEE-ray eez-E-nah dah)

GALICIAN *
Chámome [your name]
(chah-MO-may)

VALENCIAN *
A mi me diuen [your name]
(ah mee may DE-oo-en)

CATALAN *
Em dic [your name]
(em-dees)

* official co-languages

In Barcelona, I am meeting up with my good buddy Javier. His dad was one of my college soccer coaches. He is as crazy about this beautiful game as I am. Javier is lucky to live here, where soccer—called *fútbol (foot-BALL)*—is the national sport.

"The Primera División (First Division) of the pro league in Spain is called La Liga. It is one of the best in the world."

WORDS 2 KNOW

legendary: very famous.

essence: most important feature.

There are two major teams in Spain: Real Madrid *(ray-AHL MAH-dreed)* and FC Barcelona. Javier has hinted we might get to see these **legendary** teams play. This would be a dream come true.

THE FLAG OF SPAIN

Spain's flag is made up of three horizontal stripes: red, yellow, and red. The yellow stripe is exactly double the size of one red stripe. The royal seal is on the left side of the flag.

This flag was created in 1783 when King Charles III had a contest to design a new flag. He wanted the flag to stand out, since most other European flags had lots of white. This made it harder to tell them apart, especially at sea.

The colors don't officially represent anything. Some people feel the red is for bravery and yellow is for generosity.

Javier has planned the trip of a lifetime. We will explore the amazing mountains of Spain and even try to see one of the rarest animals on Earth. I hope to experience the **essence** of Spanish culture—to celebrate each day to the fullest.

It looks like we are about to dock. I better start practicing how to introduce myself in all the different languages!

SPANISH AUTONOMOUS COMMUNITIES

There are 17 autonomous communities in Spain. Even though they are part of Spain, each has its own local government. Many have their own language and customs. Go to a map of Spain and try to find each of these communities and where it is located.

1. ANDALUSIA
2. ARAGON
3. PRINCIPALITY OF ASTURIUS
4. BALEARIC ISLANDS
5. BASQUE COUNTRY
6. CANARY ISLANDS
7. CANTABRIA
8. CASTILE-LA MANCHA
9. CASTILE AND LEÓN
10. CATALONIA
11. EXTRAMADURA
12. GALICIA
13. LA RIOJA
14. MADRID
15. REGION OF MURCIA
16. FLORAL COMMUNITY OF NAVARRE
17. VALENCIAN COMMUNITY

COMMUNITY UNITY

Create your very own community just like one in Spain.

1 Decide on a name for your community. Be creative. It can come from where you live or your family name, or even the kind of animals you like.

2 Draw a flag for your new community. The stars on the American flag represent the 50 states. What do your symbols stand for on your flag?

3 Make up your own community language. Name it and decide what's different about it. You can add a letter or sound to every word or sing or whisper your language.

4 Finally, pick your national sport. This can be real, like soccer or baseball. Or it can be totally silly—like plastic duck racing or whipped cream eating.

SUPPLIES

◊ art supplies
◊ art paper
◊ notebook
◊ pen or pencil

BARCELONA AND BEYOND

From the ramp at the dock, I can see my friend Javier and his family. We wave hello. When I finally get on solid land, my legs feel all wobbly!

First I use the traditional Spanish greeting of a kiss on both cheeks to everyone in the family. Then, before I forget, I bring out my soccer ball so that Javier can be the first to sign it. I am planning to have the ball signed wherever we go as a souvenir of this adventure.

Rough seas made the ship over an hour late. I can only imagine what it was like 2,000 years ago when people were exploring this land in ancient boats. As we drive to Javier's house, I apologize for making everyone late for dinner.

"*El paseo* means 'the walk.' It is the time at night when family and friends gather and connect as they stroll along the local streets."

Javier grins. He thought for sure I knew that Spanish people are famous for staying up late. The big meal of the day is lunch. A light dinner happens later in the evening, usually following *el paseo (el pah-SAY-o).*

After dropping off my luggage, Javier and I start *el paseo* on La Rambla. This is one of the most famous streets in Spain.

I love being in the crowd. Since my Spanish is not so great, I use my soccer ball to make friends and say hello. People always pass it back to me, with a smile and a wave.

Each section of the walk has different shops, from pets to food to flowers. Along the way we see street performers: human statues, musicians, dancers, and fortune tellers. We stop at a **Tarot card** reader. She tells us that she sees a big soccer game in our future.

Did the ball give it away?

WORDS 2 KNOW

Tarot cards: special cards used to tell fortunes.

Finally we reach La Boqueria, one of the largest outdoor markets in Europe. There is so much great food. I see everything from unusual cheeses and fresh meats to refreshing fruit drinks.

My stomach is grumbling so loud it sounds like one of the drummers we heard on the street, and I'm excited to try everything. I am one hungry traveler! Javier tells me we will stop at a restaurant where his family knows the chef.

As we step inside the dining room, the most delicious smell hits my nose. The chef invites us to the kitchen where we get to help him make paella (*pie-YAH*). This traditional rice dish made with a spice called saffron is served all over the country. Our paella has chicken, seafood, and vegetables.

"Everyone has their own style of making paella, just like your mom might have her special recipe for chocolate chip cookies."

Finally we sit down to eat. If I was at home I would never have tried this food. But here in Spain, I want to take advantage of every minute the day has to offer. I don't want to regret that I didn't try or do something special.

"As they say in Spain, *buen provecho (boo-EN pro-VAY-cho)!* **Enjoy your meal!"**

The first dish is soup—but it's ice cold. I feel embarrassed to say anything, so I quietly try to get the waiter's attention. Javier laughs. The soup is gazpacho *(gath-PAH-cho)*, and it is supposed to be cold! It seems funny to eat cold soup . . . but it's delicious. When the paella comes it tastes as good as it looks.

As we eat, Javier tells me we are visiting some incredible sites in Barcelona tomorrow. We'll end the day at Camp Nou. This is the soccer stadium that is home to FC Barcelona.

FIESTA TIME

A fiesta *(fee-ESS-tah)* is a festival with many ways of celebrating. I like the castellers tradition the most. Teams challenge each other to see who can build the biggest human tower. They each stand on their shoulders going higher and higher. Remember, they are experts, so don't try this at home!

GITANOS

Remember the Tarot card reader who read our cards on La Rambla? Her ancestors are Romani people whose name is Gitano. They often move from place to place, and do not become part of the community for long. They speak their own language, Romaní.

The Gitanos came 1,000 years ago from the area that is now India. Over time they made their way through Europe. Although fortune telling is one of their traditions, the most famous part of Gitano culture is flamenco dance and flamenco music. This is a combination of Arabic, Moorish, and Jewish folk music influences. Flamenco is known for its fast rhythms. See if you can find a video of flamenco dancing or music on the Internet.

Today there are many famous Gitanos, from singers and flamenco guitarists to soccer players!

NOW AND THEN

I will learn a lot about the different people that have lived in Spain because of what they left behind—from art and buildings to writings and customs. If you wanted someone in the future to know about your life and your family, what would you leave behind?

1 Ask each member of your family to pick three objects that represent your life together. Remember, you are going to put these in a container for many years, so make sure it's something that you won't miss. It can be anything from a favorite toy or a photo to an empty box or wrapper of your favorite food.

2 Have each person write a letter about the objects. The letter should describe what the objects represent about your life.

SUPPLIES

◊ objects to put in a time capsule

◊ paper and pen

◊ plastic or metal box that can withstand being in the dirt

3 Put the objects and letters in the box and seal it up. Mark it on the outside with your family name and the words "Time Capsule."

4 Select a time you are going to open it—five years from now? Ten? When you are 21? Select a spot to keep your time capsule. It can go in a closet or, if you are more adventurous, bury it in the backyard!

Time Capsule

A NOU DAY

Javier wakes me early for a traditional small breakfast with his family. His parents have a roll and *café con leche (cah-FAY kon LAY-chay).* This is coffee with steamed milk. We have a roll and some cheese. It's the perfect start for the big day we have ahead, exploring some famous sites in the city.

First we'll visit the Palau Reial Major and Musea D'Historia de la Ciutat. These are the Royal Palace and the City History Museum. The Royal Palace is where Queen Isabella may have welcomed Columbus home from the New World. It is cool to stand in a place with so much history.

The museum has many interesting exhibits, but also a buried secret. It is built on top of the ancient Roman ruins of a city called Barcino. An elevator with a digital clock counts down the years as you go down. The doors open to a world that existed 1,400 years ago!

We get to walk through the ruins of the ancient streets. This is so much fun. I wonder what I would have been doing on these streets if I was really able to time travel. Do you think soccer was invented yet?

THE ARTISTS OF SPAIN

Spain is home to some of the world's most famous artists. Pablo Picasso, Antoni Gaudi, Salvador Dali, and Joan Miro are all from Spain. Here is an example of one of Dali's paintings.

Next we visit Park Güell. This big city park was designed by Antoni Gaudi in the 1800s. It's like stepping into a fairy tale. There are giant **ceramic** animals and a **mosaic** serpent bench. Buildings with bending columns and curved roofs remind me of sand-drip castles. We spot some green birds called monk parakeets and hummingbirds flying around.

The park is so interesting I almost forget about this afternoon. We're going to Camp Nou, Barcelona's football stadium. It seats over 99,000 people, making it the largest stadium in Europe.

As we tour the stadium and trophy room, Javier explains the **rivalry** between FC Barcelona and Real Madrid. Barcelona is in Catalonia and Madrid is in the Madrid region. Each area has its own identity and traditions and is full of pride. So winning the game takes on a bigger meaning.

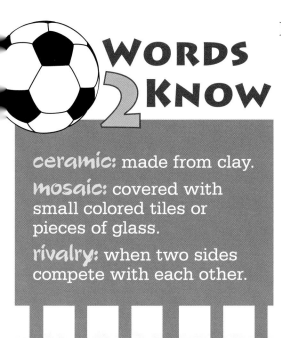

WORDS 2 KNOW

ceramic: made from clay.

mosaic: covered with small colored tiles or pieces of glass.

rivalry: when two sides compete with each other.

Millions of fans look forward to the two teams playing twice a year, called *El Clásico (el KLAH-see-co)*.

Javier's dad is a club member of FC Barcelona. Because of his dad's membership, we get to have a meal with some of the famous former players.

It means so much to meet all these great players. Still, I secretly wish I could see the team play in person at their Madrid game in two days. Javier breaks into a grin. We will be at that game! I am so excited I don't think I will sleep tonight.

"Can you think of two other sports teams that have such a strong rivalry?"

MR. SANDMAN

Many of the materials that Gaudi and other architects use depend on solids mixing with water, like plaster, glue, cement, and paint. This is due to **surface tension** since the water **molecules** like to stick together.

Remember how I said Gaudi's architecture looked like sand drip castles? This fun (but messy) science project will help you understand surface tension.

1 Put the bowl on the tarp or in the box. Fill your measuring cup with sand and pour it in the bowl.

2 Add 1 tablespoon of water to the sand and mix. Is the sand sticking together enough to build a castle? If not, continue adding tablespoons of water until the mixture is perfect for building. In your notebook, write down what you observe.

SUPPLIES

◊ large bowl
◊ box or tarp
◊ measuring cup
◊ sand from the beach or gardening supply store
◊ tablespoon
◊ water
◊ old spoon or mixing tool
◊ notebook
◊ pencil

WORDS 2 KNOW

3 Now keep adding water until the sand becomes more like a mud or a thick liquid.

surface tension: the way molecules of a liquid stick together and form the smallest surface area.

molecule: the smallest amount of something.

The drier the sand, the less surface tension there is. The perfect surface tension is reached when the water sticks to the sand. When is the sand too dry to stick together? At what point is it perfect for molding sand castles? When does it become so watery that it doesn't hold together?

DRIP CASTLE

Create your own fantastic castle like Gaudi. Once the castle is done, take handfuls of the wet sand. While holding it in your fist, slowly let it drip onto the castle from above.

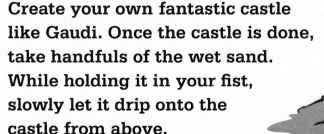

MADRID MANIA

We wake up early and drive to the beautiful Barcelona train station. Javier's family is all wearing the traditional colors of FC Barcelona—blue and maroon. Each team has one set of colors for home games and a different set for away games. The away game colors can change from year to year.

Madrid Mania

avier wants me to wear FC Barcelona colors, too. But I like both teams. So I decide to just wear the Spanish colors of red and yellow. This way I can't lose. Javier jokes that he will still sit with me!

We board an AVE train, a high-speed train that will take us to Madrid in under three hours. Our top speed will reach over 180 miles per hour! The train's front is shaped like a duck beak because this shape cuts through the air well.

Javier and I watch the scenery flash by and talk about how much he loves school. He reminds me that Madrid is both the name of the community and the city. Madrid is one of the largest cities in Europe.

FIESTA TIME

Madrid's most famous fiesta honors the city's patron saint, Saint Isidore. For nine days in May, the San Isidro fiesta has bullfighting celebrations and fireworks. Residents dress in traditional folk costumes.

The Madrid train station holds many surprises. Their are indoor gardens and ponds with fish and turtles. And Javier's older cousin Sophia is waiting there for us. She is dressed in Real Madrid's colors of white and blue! I am glad I am staying **neutral** for this game.

Santiago Bernabéu—the stadium of over 80,000 seats—has a lot of history. Finals for the UEFA European Championships and even a FIFA World Cup (1982) have been hosted here. This is where Spain's National Team plays many of its matches against other countries. So it's safe to say that the Spanish team who won the 2010 FIFA World Cup played here!

As the game begins I can feel the excitement in the air. I am just happy to cheer both teams.

WORDS 2 KNOW

neutral: not taking a side.
mimic: to copy the actions of something.
matador: the main bullfighter in a bullfight.

The soccer teams battle, with Real Madrid winning 2–1. Javier jokingly blames it on the fact that I didn't wear the right colors! He is sure FC Barcelona will win next time.

"Soccer is about bringing people together and doing your best."

At dinner there are some amazing dancers as part of a dinner show. A man and a woman do the *paso doble (PAH-so DOUGH-bleh)*. This dance **mimics** the powerful moves of a bullfighter. Usually the woman is the cape and the man is the bullfighter. It is very intense, even more so when the dancer asks me to come up on stage and try my hand at being the **matador**.

Everyone in the restaurant cheers me on. Even though I am very bad at it, I couldn't think of a better way to end the most incredible day. Except to say: *ole! (o-LAY)*. This is an expression of being excited, like when we yell "hooray!" or "yippee!"

IT'S ELECTRIC

The super-fast AVE trains in Spain run on electricity. Here is a simple electricity experiment to do with an adult.

1 Put your palm on top of the lemon and roll it back and forth a few times to help the lemon become more juicy.

2 Be sure to wash the coins thoroughly with hot water and antibacterial soap.

3 Ask an adult to carve two slots into the lemon, side by side. They need to be just far enough apart so that the coins do not touch each other. Then place one coin into each of the slots in the lemon.

SUPPLIES

◊ lemon
◊ hot water
◊ antibacterial soap
◊ sharp knife
◊ dime
◊ penny
◊ glass of warm water

4 Make sure your tongue is wet with saliva and—yes, that's right!—put it between the coins so that each side of your tongue touches a coin. You should feel a tingling sensation. This is actually a small electric current! Rinse your mouth out with warm water when you are finished.

The acid in the lemon juice reacts to the different metals in the dime and penny. One is a positive charge and one is a negative charge. When you put your tongue between the coins, you complete the circuit so that the charge travels!

FIESTA TIME

The community of Buñol has an annual fiesta called La Tomatina. I bet you guessed that it has to do with tomatoes. In fact, it is one big hour-long food fight. Thousands of people come to throw tomatoes at each other!

RARE EARTH

Today's adventure could be a once-in-a-lifetime experience. Javier wants to see an Iberian lynx, one of the rarest animals on the planet. There are less than 100 alive, so it is nearly **extinct**. It does mean taking a four-hour, guided park tour by off-road vehicle. "What if we don't see it?" he asks.

We've talked about Spanish culture and living for the moment. This is one of those times, because this chance may not happen again. If we don't try, then we definitely will not see the lynx. Besides, we will have a good time no matter what.

On our way, we stop in the small town of Palos de la Frontera. This is where Columbus set sail for the New World with three ships, the *Niña*, *Pinta*, and *Santa Maria*. Two of his captains—the Pinzón brothers—lived here. It's amazing to think how one explorer's adventure could change history.

Columbus took a huge risk to explore the world. Imagine if he didn't follow his dreams? Javier and I pretend we are the brothers setting sail, arguing about what to pack as we nibble on the local treat of *polvorón (pol-vo-RONE)*. These are shortbread-like cookies.

WORDS 2 KNOW

extinct: when an animal or plant no longer exists.

"It's good to have dreams. Aim high and shoot for the stars."

We head south to Doñana National Park. This **World Heritage site** is a protected **wetlands** area. It covers over 123,000 acres of marsh, scrublands, and sand dunes. These are very important wildlife **habitats**.

The tour starts with an off-road ride into the park. Our guide Luis signs my ball and speaks enough English to say "I love soccer, too!" Javier translates it back in Spanish: "Me encanta el fútbol también *(may en-CAHN-tah el foot-BALL tam-be-EN)*."

WORDS 2 KNOW

World Heritage site: a special place named by the United Nations that deserves to be protected.

wetlands: low areas filled with water, such as a marsh or swamp.

habitat: the natural area where an animal lives.

The hours go by quickly because we spot all sorts of remarkable animals—flamingoes, red deer, and wild boars. Then our guide finally pulls to a stop where the lynx has been spotted before.

We get very quiet, take out our binoculars and wait, and wait, and wait. After 10 minutes turns into 20, everyone begins to fidget . . . and then Luis signals to us with his hands. There, frozen in place, is an Iberian lynx with its tuft ears and leopard-like spots. He stares right back at us.

"It almost feels like the lynx is saying: 'please protect me and all animals for future generations.'"

A few days later we take another journey, this time even farther south. To pass the time in the car, Javier challenges me with a riddle. How can we go to Great Britain while we are still in Spain?

Remember how I told you that there are some Spanish cities located in North Africa and a Spanish village in France? Gibraltar, on a peninsula on the tip of southern Spain, is part of Great Britain. You could fit seven Gibraltars on Manhattan in New York.

FIESTA TIME

In Andalusia, they hold a fiesta called the Celebration of the River Guadalquivir. One of the main events is racing horses along the beach. It is a thrilling sight.

The Rock of Gibraltar is an enormous mass of rock. It steeply rises 1,400 feet (425 meters) above the sea. When we arrive, we get to see its caves, fortresses, and tunnels. Javier promises me we will see more animals, too.

The ride up the Rock of Gibraltar in a cable car is breathtaking. We get off at Middle Station, and come face to face with wild, tailless monkeys called Barbary Macaques. People are not allowed to touch the animals or feed them, but they can touch us.

As I am looking at the view to the ocean below, one of them comes up and starts playing with my curly hair. "He probably thinks we are brothers," Javier says, laughing. I'm glad he got a picture so I can show everyone back home.

ANIMALS ROCK

Just like the Iberian lynx, there may be animals in your area that face a tough survival battle. Since we just finished visiting a big rock, we can learn about these animals and do a rock art project at the same time.

1. Go online or to the library and research endangered animals in your state. You can also call your state's wildlife organization to find out about animals that are struggling to survive in your area.

2. Choose an animal for your rock art project. Outline the animal on your rock with black marker or black paint. Then color it in like you would a coloring book. Let it dry overnight.

3. Show your family and friends your rock. Tell them about the animal you chose and its struggle to survive.

SUPPLIES

◊ rock with a smooth surface
◊ paint or markers

YOU'RE A NATURAL

Today we are flying to northern Spain to experience some of the country's most magnificent mountains. Did you know that Spain is the most mountainous country in Europe after Switzerland? We are heading to the beautiful Picos range for a hike on Desfiladero del Rio Cares.

You're A Natural

This walk follows the river Cares and a manmade canal. For part of the trip, there is a 300-foot drop next to the path. It's a good thing I am not afraid of heights!

Some of the path is carved right into the walls of the mountains. We pass rock formations and simple old cottages where the workers who built the canals used to live. There are even small tunnels with waterfalls on the other side.

After two hours we come to a long tunnel where we have to use flashlights! It's like someone turned off the lights in the middle of the day. I tell Javier to make sure he doesn't bump his head. If he does, it could cause him to start rooting for Madrid!

When we reach the town at the other end, Javier's parents are there to meet us.

A few days later, I join Javier's family for one more trip before I leave this beautiful country. We are flying to the Canary Islands. The seven main islands are to the south of Spain off the coast of Africa. To get to one of them, Tenerife, we are cruising by **hydrofoil**. A guide named Matteo shows us a very rare, odd-looking tree. Ancient people used to think the sap had healing properties.

Next we see the stunning **volcanic** landscape of Parque Nacional de Teide. The lava rock in this area is over 180,000 years old, with strange-looking formations. They are a reminder of the incredible power of nature.

"The land makes me feel like we are on a different planet."

It makes my trip to Spain seem like a blip on the planet's clock. I am sad to be leaving tomorrow. But saying goodbye just means I get to come back again soon.

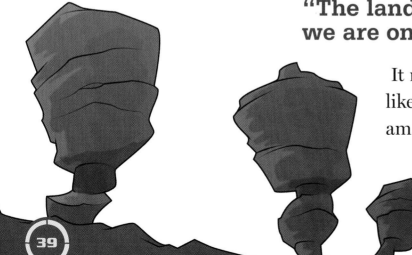

SILBO GOMERO

Matteo is from the island of La Gomera, famous for its ancient whistle language called Silbo Gomero. Because of the geography and acoustics of the island, people speak by whistles instead of words.

Changes in pitch, duration, and volume create different meanings. Can you think of another form of expression like this? That's right, music!

It reminds me of our South Africa adventure and the languages that use mouth clicks. Matteo whistles, "Ethan, welcome to the island!" I'm definitely going to practice my whistling when I get back home.

WORDS 2 KNOW

hydrofoil: a fast boat that skims on top of the water.

volcanic: from lava that came out of a volcano.

geography: the features of a place, such as mountains and rivers.

acoustics: the way sound carries within a space.

pitch: how high or low a sound is.

duration: how long something lasts.

volume: how loud a sound is.

LOVE THE LAVA

In this project, you are going to make a volcano that actually erupts with "lava." Have an adult supervise.

1 Place the box or tray on the tarp or newspaper. Stand the bottle up in the box or on the tray.

2 Mix the flour, salt, oil, and water into a dough in the bowl. Mold the salt dough around the bottle, making a volcano shape around it. Make sure you don't get any dough in the opening.

3 Using the funnel, fill the bottle halfway with the warm water. Squirt a few drops of red food coloring in the water. Pour in the baking soda and the dishwashing liquid.

SUPPLIES

◊ box or cardboard tray

◊ tarp or newspaper

◊ empty 2-liter soda bottle

◊ 6 cups flour

◊ 2 cups salt

◊ 4 tablespoons vegetable oil

◊ 2 cups water

◊ bowl and spoon

◊ funnel

◊ warm water

◊ red food coloring

◊ 2 tablespoons baking soda

◊ a few drops of dishwashing liquid

◊ ½ cup white vinegar

4 Now for the fun part! Using the funnel, pour in the vinegar and step back. Your volcano will erupt with lava.

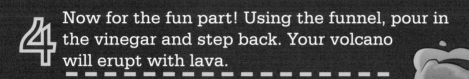

How does this work? The reaction between vinegar and baking soda makes a gas called carbon dioxide. When gas builds up it has to go somewhere, which makes the "lava" erupt. This is what happens with real lava too.

FIESTA TIME

Santa Cruz de Tenerife has one of the biggest Carnival celebrations in the world. It is sort of like Mardi Gras in New Orleans. There are street festivals, people dressed in costume, and my favorite silly event of all: the Burial of the Sardine. A giant papier mâché model of a sardine is carried through the streets. Everyone pretends to mourn and cry along the way.

THE LONG GOODBYE

N ow it is time to say goodbye to this fascinating country. I've seen rare animals and where Columbus began his journey. From wild soccer classicos to eating gazpacho and paella, Javier has given me many wonderful memories.

I have learned so much about this country and the Spanish culture. Most importantly, I have adopted the spirit of enjoying every single moment, and feeling connected to a bigger family. I will take this outlook on life to every *Soccer World* destination I visit.

As with all of my adventures, the trip would not be complete without trading gifts. I give Javier a string bracelet from our last trip in Mexico, and something he was not expecting . . . my signed soccer ball.

WHERE NEXT?

Where do you want to go for our next soccer adventure? Email me at Ethan@soccerworldadventure.com to share your ideas.

The Long Goodbye

"I ask Javier to take my signed soccer ball with him wherever he goes, and pass it along to other friends around the world."

Javier gives me a beautiful Spanish guitar. He tells me it was his father's when he was a young boy, and that I should definitely practice my singing.

We hug again and I bid farewell to this nation of World Cup champions. I wonder where we will land next. Stay tuned . . .

GIVE BACK TO SPAIN

In each and every country we visit together, I challenge you to find a give back project. You can research ideas on the Internet and write a letter. If your parents approve, do a fundraiser like a bake sale or a car wash or whatever you like.

You can email me and let me know about your projects!

GLOSSARY

acoustics: the way sound carries within a space.

autonomous: independent.

ceramic: made from clay.

culture: the beliefs and customs of a group of people.

customs: ways of doing things.

democracy: government elected freely by the people.

duration: how long something lasts.

essence: most important feature.

extinct: when an animal or plant no longer exists.

geography: the features of a place, such as mountains and rivers.

habitat: the natural area where an animal lives.

hydrofoil: a fast boat that skims on top of the water.

legendary: very famous.

matador: the main bullfighter in a bullfight.

mimic: to copy the actions of something.

molecule: the smallest amount of something.

mosaic: covered with small colored tiles or pieces of glass.

neutral: not taking a side.

peninsula: a piece of land that juts out into water.

Phoenicians: people who explored the Mediterranean Sea 3,000 years ago.

pitch: how high or low a sound is.

port: a harbor where ships can load and unload.

province: part of a country.

rivalry: when two sides compete with each other.

surface tension: the way molecules of a liquid stick together and form the smallest surface area.

Tarot cards: special cards used to tell fortunes.

traditions: customs handed down over time.

volcanic: from lava that came out of a volcano.

volume: how loud a sound is.

wetlands: low areas filled with water, such as a marsh or swamp.

World Heritage site: a special place named by the United Nations that deserves to be protected.

INDEX